KINDERGARTEN THINKING SKILLS

Fun-filled Activities

Connect The Halves

Colour the two halves with same colour crayon and match them using a line.

   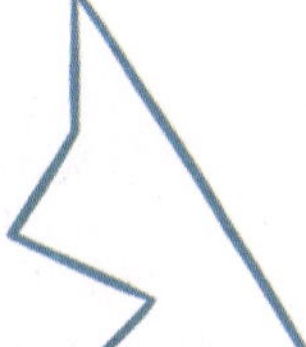

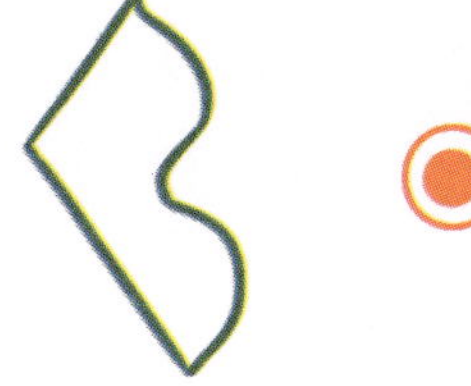  

  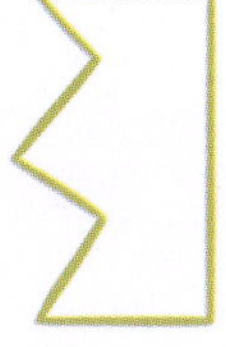

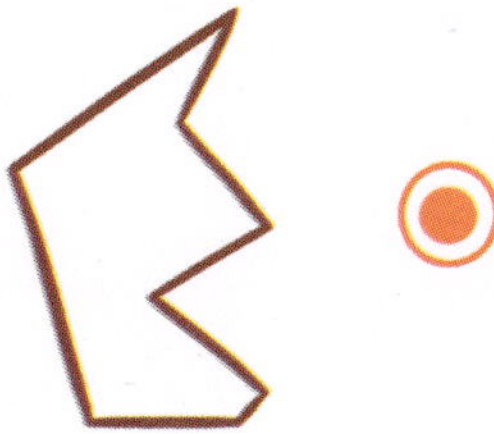  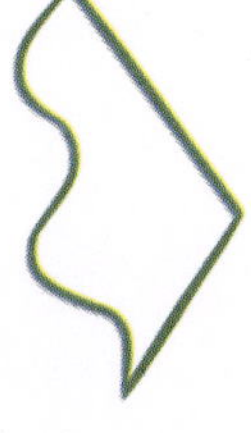

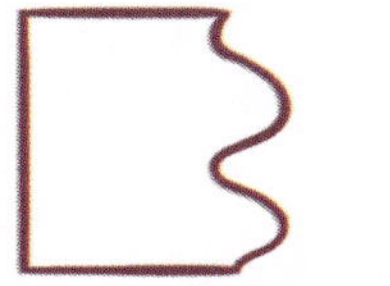  

The Other Half!

Colour the two halves of each fruit with the same colour.

Butterfly Match

Find the butterfly that has the same pattern as the one on the top. Draw a line to connect the two matching butterflies.

Match Me To The Yarn

Help each cat reach the yarn. Write its number in the correct circle.

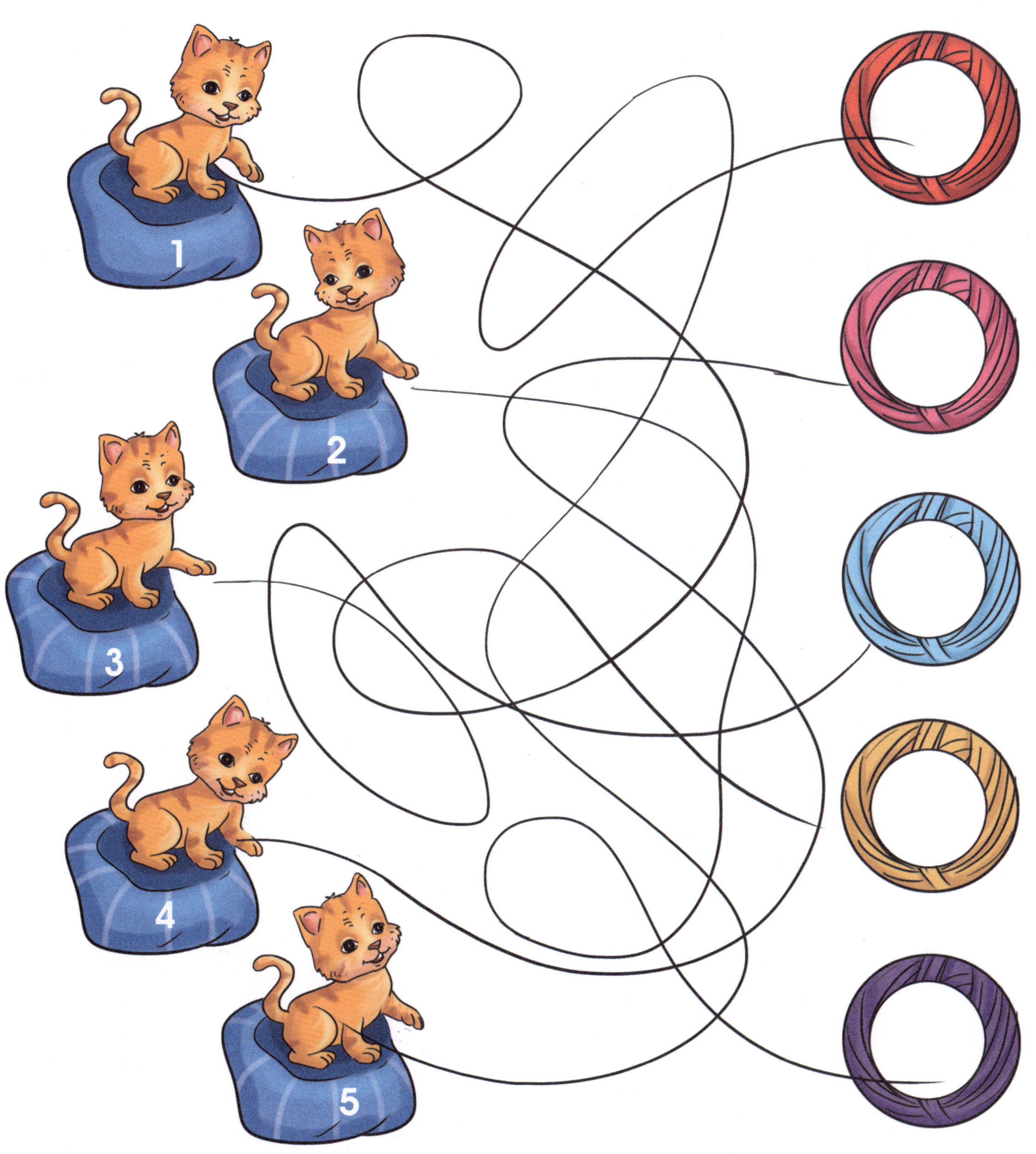

Number Maze

The bus needs to get to school through the number path. Colour the boxes from number 1-10 to help the bus reach the school.

SCHOOL BUS		8	7	6	5
		1	2	3	9
3	9	5	8	4	1
1	10	7	6	5	3
4	6	8	3	SCHOOL	
5	2	9	10		

Fast And Safe

Find the fastest and safest way for Mac to reach home.

Same Group

Circle (O) the pictures that are of the same group as the first one in each row.

Same Group

Draw a circle (O) around the picture that has something in common with the first picture.

What Is It?

Circle (O) the picture in each row that is described by the words above the box.

big green sleeping

cold soft sweet

loud happy musical

small red tasty

What Is It?

Circle (O) the correct picture by following the word clues.

1. red, small seeds outside, stem with green leaves

2. round, rough outer skin, orange

3. red, green or yellow, used to make cider

4. round and shiny, one seed at its core

5. long and slender, yellow when ripe, you peel its skin to eat it

Left And Right

Read the instruction given below the shapes and colour them accordingly.

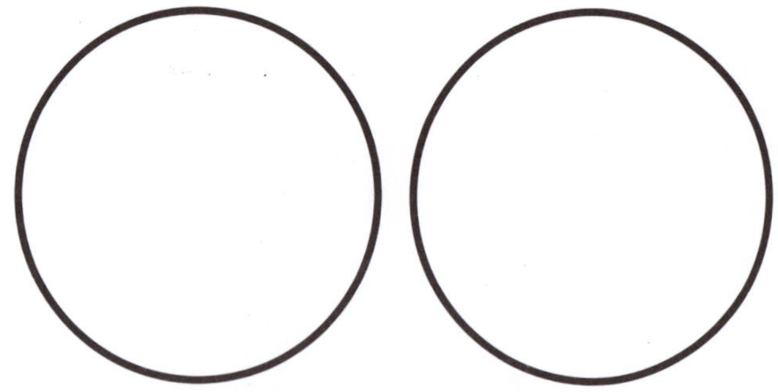

Colour the RIGHT circle RED

Colour the LEFT square GREEN

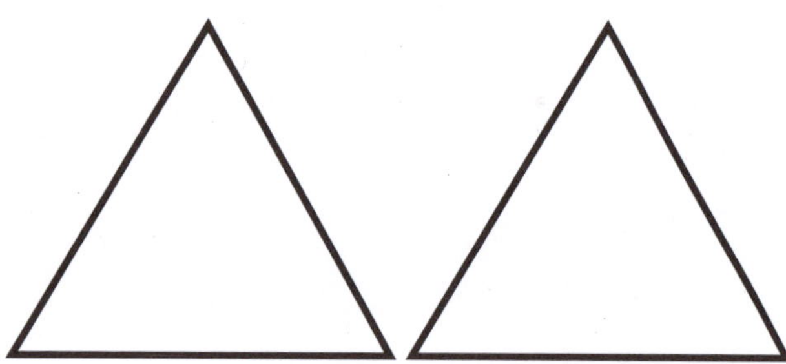

Colour the LEFT triangle BLUE

Colour the RIGHT star YELLOW

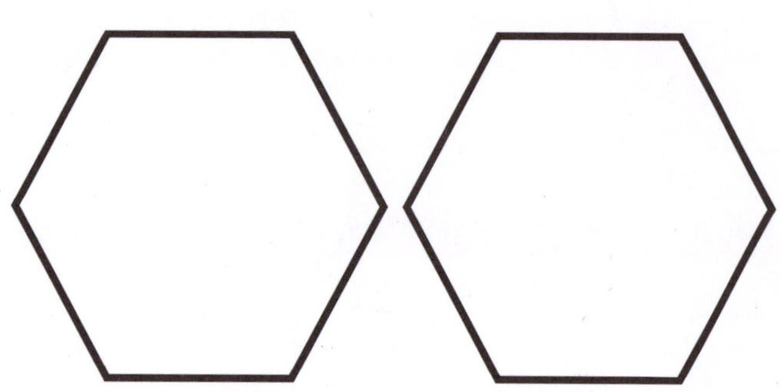

Colour the RIGHT hexagon ORANGE

Colour the RIGHT diamond PINK

Think And Do

Read, follow the directions and draw the pictures in the correct boxes below.

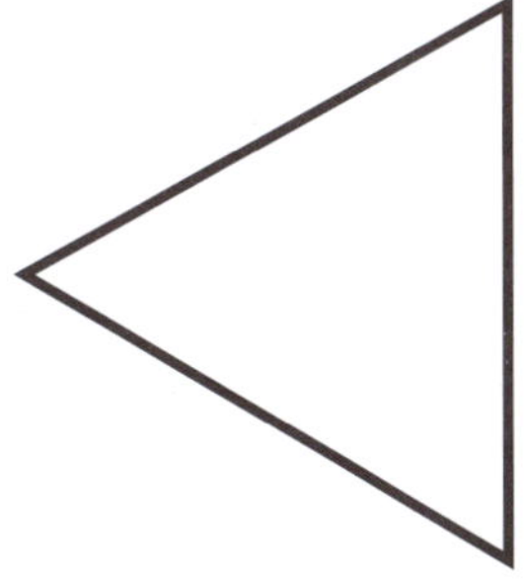

1. The **ball** is on the **left.**
2. The **kite** is on the **right.**
3. Where is the plane?

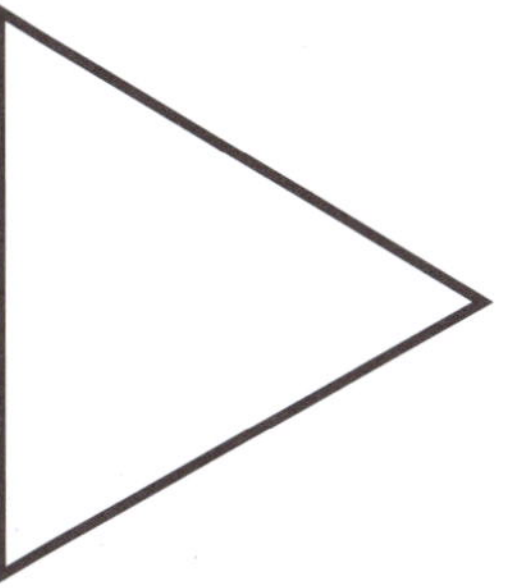

What Should I Use?

Draw a line from the children to the object they should use for the activities shown below.

Find The Correct Shadow

Draw a line to match the shadow with the correct picture.

Shape Match

Look at the drawings Teddy has made. Draw a line from the drawings to the shapes they are made of.

What Is Different?

Find 5 differences between the two pictures.

Blow With The Wind

Colour the things that will blow in the wind.

Draw two things that can fly.

What Is Wrong?

Circle (O) the things that are wrong in the picture.

The boy is wearing an apron while cycling. Is it correct? What should the boy wear then? Draw here.

Seek And Find

Find the hidden objects in the picture and circle (O) them.

Match The Correct Animal

Draw lines to match the front and back facing pictures of these animals.

Patterns

Shade the shapes and complete the patterns.

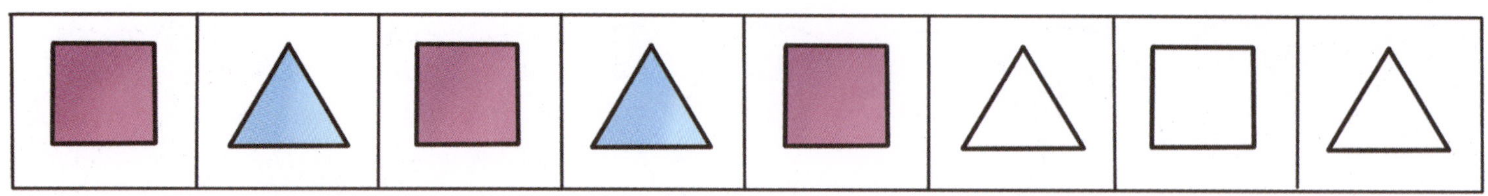

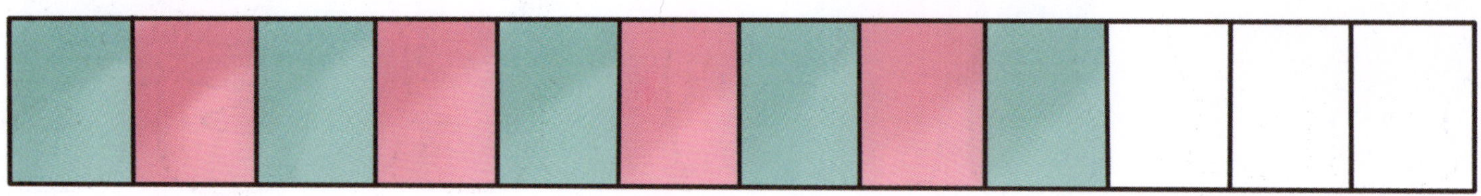

Colour Clues

Look at the picture clues and colour the aliens. How many of each are there?

How Many?

How many fruits does Suzy have? Colour the fruits with different crayons and find for yourself!

What Comes Next?

Draw a line from each picture on the left to the pictures on the right to show what happens next.

What Comes Next?

Draw a line from each picture on the left to the pictures on the right to show what happens next.

Tim Wins The Race!

Put these pictures in the right order to make a story. Write 1, 2, 3 and 4 in the boxes.

Kate Made A Picture

Put these pictures in right order to show how Kate drew a picture. Write 1, 2, 3 and 4 in the boxes.

What Happened?

Why is the girl scared? Circle (O) the picture which shows why.

ANSWER KEY

Page 2

Page 3

Children will do on their own.

Page 4

Page 5

Children will do on their own.

Page 6

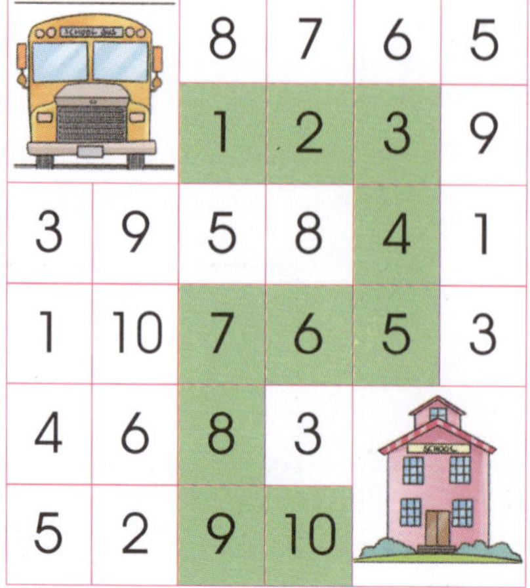

Page 7

Page 8

Page 9

Page 10

Page 11

ANSWER KEY

Page 12

Children will do on their own.

Page 13

Children will do on their own.

Page 14

Page 15

Page 16

Page 17

Page 18

Children should colour balloon, feather, paper plane and kite

Page 19

These things are wrong:

1. Giraffe cooking
2. Girl wearing sports shoes
3. Books on kitchen shelf
4. Boy wearing apron on the bicycle
5. Blackboard in the picture

Page 20

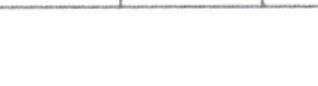

Page 21

Page 22

Children will do on their own

ANSWER KEY

Page 23

Children will do on their own

Page 24

Children will colour on their own- the fruits are cherry, apple, banana, pear and pomegranate

Page 25

Page 26

Page 27

The correct order is- 2, 4, 1 and 3

Page 28

Page 29